The Dollmaker's Ghost

Larry Levis

The
Dollmaker's
Ghost

Carnegie Mellon University Press

Pittsburgh 1992

Grateful acknowledgment is made to W. W. Norton and Company, Inc. for permission to quote from *The Letters of Rainer Maria Rilke 1892–1910* translated by Jane Bannard Greene and M. D. Herter Norton. Copyright 1945 W. W. Norton & Company, renewed 1972 M. D. Herter Norton.

Library of Congress Catalog Card Number 91-70995
ISBN 0-88748-282-1

First Carnegie Mellon University Press Edition,
February 1992

The Dollmaker's Ghost was first published by E.P. Dutton,
New York, in 1981.

Publication of this book is supported by gifts to the Classic Contemporaries Series from James W. Hall, Richard M. Cyert, and other anonymous benefactors.

For Marcia and Nicholas

Had I been able to make *the fears I experienced thus, had I been able to shape things out of them, real, still things that it is serenity and freedom to create and from which, when they exist, reassurance emanates, then nothing would have happened to me. But these fears that fell to my lot out of every day stirred a hundred other fears, and they stood up in me against me and agreed among themselves, and I couldn't get beyond them. In striving to form them, I came to work creatively on* them; *instead of making them into things of my will, I only gave them a life of their own which they turned against me and with which they pursued me far into the night. Had things been better with me, more quiet and friendly, had my room stood by me, and had I remained well, perhaps I would have been able to do it even so: to make things out of fear. . . .*

For, see, I am a stranger and a poor man. And I shall pass.

*—Rainer Maria Rilke, from a
letter to Lou Andreas-Salomé, Worpswede bei
Bremen, July 18, 1903.*

Contents

Part Four

Acknowledgments

I would like to thank the editors of the following magazines in which these poems previously appeared:

The American Poetry Review: "For a Ghost Who Once Placed Bets in the Park."

Antaeus: "Edward Hopper, *Hotel Room*, 1931"; "García Lorca: A Photograph of the Granada Cemetery, 1966"; "The Grass"; "Ice"; "For Miguel Hernández in His Sleep and in His Sickness: Spring, 1942, Madrid"; "Lost Fan, Hotel Californian, Fresno, 1923"; "Magnolia"; "Overhearing the Dollmaker's Ghost on the Riverbank"; "Some Ashes Drifting Above Piedra, California."

The Chariton Review: "A Study of Three Crows."

Crazy Horse: "The Blue Hatband."

Field: "Blue Stones"; "For Zbigniew Herbert, Summer, 1971, Los Angeles"; "The Future of Hands"; "The Ownership of the Night"; "Words for the Axe."

The Georgia Review: "The Wish to Be Picked Clean."

The Iowa Review: "Adah."

New Letters: "My Only Photograph of Weldon Kees."

The New Yorker: "Picking Grapes in an Abandoned Vineyard." © 1980 The New Yorker Magazine, Inc.

Ploughshares: Section 1 of "A Pool of Light," under the title "Silk."

Poetry: "To a Wall of Flame in a Steel Mill, Syracuse, New York, 1969"; "To a Woman Glancing Up from the River."

Poet's Choice: "Blue Stones."

Porch: Section 2 of "A Pool of Light," under the title, "A Painting Full of Clouds above the Deathbed of My Grandmother, Huntington Lake, California."

The Pushcart Prize IV: Best of the Small Presses: "The Ownership of the Night."

Sky Writing: "Story."

I would like to thank the University of Missouri for a Summer Research Grant in 1979 which enabled me to complete this book.

My special thanks to Philip Levine and Marcia Southwick for their constant help and understanding.

PART ONE

Picking Grapes in an
Abandoned Vineyard

Picking grapes alone in the late autumn sun—
A short, curved knife in my hand,
Its blade silver from so many sharpenings,
Its handle black.
I still have a scar where a friend
Sliced open my right index finger, once,
In a cutting shed—
The same kind of knife.
The grapes drop into the pan,
And the gnats swarm over them, as always.
Fifteen years ago,
I worked this row of vines beside a dozen
Families up from Mexico.
No one spoke English, or wanted to.
One woman, who made an omelet with a sheet of tin
And five, light blue quail eggs,
Had a voice full of dusk, and jail cells,
And bird calls.   She spoke,
In Spanish, to no one, as they all did.
Their swearing was specific,
And polite.
I remember two of them clearly:
A man named Tea, six feet, nine inches tall
At the age of sixty-two,
Who wore white spats into downtown Fresno
Each Saturday night,
An alcoholic giant whom the women loved—
One chilled morning, they found him dead outside
The Rose Café . . .
And Angel Domínguez,

Who came to work for my grandfather in 1910,
And who saved for years to buy
Twenty acres of rotting, Thompson Seedless vines.
While the sun flared all one August,
He decided he was dying of a rare disease,
And spent his money and his last years
On specialists,
Who found nothing wrong.
Tea laughed, and, tipping back
A bottle of Muscatel, said: "Nothing's wrong.
You're just dying."
At seventeen, I discovered
Parlier, California, with its sad, topless bar,
And its one main street, and its opium.
I would stand still, and chalk my cue stick
In Johnny Palores' East Front Pool Hall, and watch
The room filling with tobacco smoke, as the sun set
Through one window.
Now all I hear are the vines rustling as I go
From one to the next,
The long canes holding up dry leaves, reddening,
So late in the year.
What the vines want must be this silence spreading
Over each town, over the dance halls and the dying parks,
And the police drowsing in their cruisers
Under the stars.
What the men who worked here wanted was
A drink strong enough
To let out what laughter they had.
I can still see the two of them:
Tea smiles and lets his yellow teeth shine—
While Angel, the serious one, for whom
Death was a rare disease,
Purses his lips, and looks down, as if
He is already mourning himself—
A soft, gray hat between his hands.
Today, in honor of them,
I press my thumb against the flat part of this blade,
And steady a bunch of red, Málaga grapes

With one hand,
The way they showed me, and cut—
And close my eyes to hear them laugh at me again,
And then, hearing nothing, no one,
Carry the grapes up into the solemn house,
Where I was born.

Wasps

In the orchards we would take
A rolled-up newspaper and light it,
And shove this torch into a wasps' nest.
In a moment the hive
Would be thick with dead wasps.
Only one or two flying out of the fire.

*

Now, when I walk in the shade of those trees,
I know they will go on dying so slowly
No one will notice.   I wish them
A long custody over the grass, because
It is easy to wish anything
For trees.

*

Today, I said I would sprawl naked,
With lips open, the sun on them,
As the world is sold to the flies,
Who sell it to the spiders and lizards.
And I will watch a lizard's throat
As it swallows perfectly, closing its eyes
Just once as it does this, then opening them.
I love the way it can do one thing well,
One thing that won't matter.

*

And if, next year, new wasps
Swarm slowly out of their hive
As usual, making one thin line of music,
While I sit listening to it,
Hearing also my neighbor slap his child
And the hush that follows,
And if I tell no one,
Will something live on inside my silence—
One black wasp unburned in a hive
Of wasps, looking like any other?

A Study of Three Crows

Three crows in a high tree
In April
Possess heaven.

It is in their black feathers
Shining like mud,
Or it is nowhere.

At the town's edge,
Where the fumes are eternal,
They feed on garbage,

Or fly up slowly,
Having fed, to overlook toys
In yards with no grass—

Their voices the sound of tools
Being sharpened
In some garage in the suburbs.

Crows are the color of soil
After long rain . . .
They strut back and forth,

Owning it all.
And their gold eyes,
When looked at closely, shine

Without any character.
They have been here a long time,
Rolling their *r*'s, and waiting.

Behind them, it is night.
The stars are
All in their places.

The Cocoon

Must have dreamed itself.

A small, gray hammock of unconcern,
It is not the witness of anything.

It waits, when it has finished,
Among hundreds just like it,

Hung in midair, in a privacy
Nothing disturbs.   This one,

So smug with its plan,
Still keeps the moisture

Of death in its fat.   It glistens,
And a thrill runs through it:

The burned, perfect face is emerging,
The serious little torso.   And this light,

This annihilation on each wing,
Seems to be singing its anthem.

It wobbles, then grows steady,
As the eyes that see nothing special

Stare at a last patch of snow.

The Future of Hands

All winter
The trees held up their silent hives
As if they mattered.
But on one main street of bars and lights,
I watched a woman who had begged for days
Throw all the coins back, insulted,
Into the crowd,
And then each cheap stone on her necklace,
As if they were confetti
At a bitter wedding,
And then her stained blouse.
I smiled, then, at her dignity.
But when the night came
With only its usual stars to show,
She was applauded and spat on,
Or those passing stepped around her,
Avoiding her body
As if it had become private, or pure.
When the police arrived,
Sniveling about the cold day she had chosen
To strip,
Her face was a brown jewel,
And I knew the hands
Of the police would have to close now,
On this body abandoned to wind,
Just as her hands closed, finally,
On wind that would have nothing
To do with her,
And never had.

*

I know that wind
Had nothing to do with longing.
I have seen that, even in the eyes
Of girls across a lunch counter—
A desire to be anywhere that wasn't

Texas, and waiting on tables—
Their eyes making a pact
With the standing, staring wheat
About to be turned back into the black soil
That spreads everywhere when no one
Is watching.

And writing this,
I stare at my hands,
Which are the chroniclers of my death,
Which pull me into this paper
Each night, as onto a bed of silk sheets,
And the woman gone.

After two hours of work,
I do not know if there ever was a woman.

I watch the flies buzz at the sill.

*

Or, if I sleep,
I must choose between two dreams.

In one of them, my hands move calmly
Over a woman's waist, or lift
In speech the way birds rise or settle
Over a marsh, over nesting places.

In the other dream,
There are no nesting places.
The birds are white, and scavenging.
They lift negligently over the town in wind,
Like paper, like the death of paper.
They dip and rise
As if there had never been a heaven.
Beneath them, it is summer.
It is the same town I was born in.
And in its one bar

The man selling illegal human hair from Mexico,
The hair of brides mixed
With the hair of the dead,
Argues all day over the price.

The Ownership of the Night

1.

After five years,
I'm in the kitchen of my parents' house
Again, hearing the aging refrigerator
Go on with its music,
And watching an insect die on the table
By turning in circles.
My face reflected in the window at night
Is paler, duller, even in summer.
And each year
I dislike sleeping a little more,
And all the hours spent
Inside something as black
As my own skull . . .
I watch
This fruit moth flutter.
Now it's stopped.

2.

Once,
Celebrating a good year for Muscatel,
My parents got away to Pismo Beach,
Shuttered and cold in the off season.
When I stare out at its surf at night,
It could be a girl in a black and white slip,
It could be nothing.
But I no longer believe this is where
America ends.   I know
It continues as oil, or sorrow, or a tiny
Island with palm trees lining
The sun baked, crumbling
Asphalt of its airstrip.
A large snake sleeps in the middle of it,
And it is not necessary to think of war,
Or the isolation of any father

Alone on a raft in the Pacific
At night, or how deep the water can get
Beneath him . . .
Not when I can think of the look of distance
That must have spread
Over my parents' faces as they
Conceived me here,
And each fell back, alone,
As the waves glinted, and fell back.

3.

This evening my thoughts
Build one white bridge after another
Into the twilight, and now the tiny couple
In the distance,
In the picture I have of them there,
This woman pregnant after a war,
And this man who whistles with a dog at his heels,
And who thinks all this is his country,
Cross over them without
Looking back, without waving.
Already, in the orchards behind them,
The solitary hives are things;
They have the dignity of things,
A gray, precise look,
While the new wasps swarm sullenly out of them,
And the trees hold up cold blossoms,
And, in the distance, the sky
Does not mind the one bird in it,
Which by now is only a frail brush stroke
On a canvas in which everything is muted and
Real.   The way laughter is real
When it ends, suddenly, between two strangers,
And you step quickly past them, into the night.

To a Wall of Flame in a Steel Mill, Syracuse, New York, 1969

Except under the cool shadows of pines,
The snow is already thawing
Along this road . . .
Such sun, and wind.
I think my father longed to disappear
While driving through this place once,
In 1957.
Beside him, my mother slept in a gray dress
While his thoughts moved like the shadow
Of a cloud over houses,
And he was seized, suddenly, by his own shyness,
By his desire to be grass,
And simplified.
Was it brought on
By the road, or the snow, or the sky
With nothing in it?
He kept sweating and wiping his face
Until it passed,
And I never knew.
But in the long journey away from my father,
I took only his silences, his indifference
To misfortune, rain, stones, music, and grief.
Now, I can sleep beside this road
If I have to,
Even while the stars pale and go out,
And it is day.
And if I can keep secrets for years,
The way a stone retains a warmth from the sun,
It is because men like us
Own nothing, really.
I remember, once,
In the steel mill where I worked,
Someone opened the door of the furnace

And I glanced in at the simple,
Quick and blank erasures the flames made of iron,
Of everything on earth.
It was reverence I felt then, and did not know why.
I do not know even now why my father
Lived out his one life
Farming two hundred acres of gray Málaga vines
And peach trees twisted
By winter.   They lived, I think,
Because his hatred of them was entire,
And wordless.
I still think of him staring into this road
Twenty years ago,
While his hands gripped the wheel harder,
And his wish to be no one made his body tremble,
Like the touch
Of a woman he could not see,
Her fingers drifting up his spine in silence
Until his loneliness was perfect,
And she let him go—
Her laughter turning into these sheets of black
And glassy ice that dislodge themselves,
And ride slowly out,
Onto the thawing river.

PART TWO

Truman, Da Vinci, Nebraska

In Kansas City, Truman is dead who ruled
In green Missouris of decisive, late
Spring nights and wet roads somebody had
To die on: between Rolla and Joplin for

A wisecrack, or a girl who stole convertibles
For thrills.   At the end I thought he'd
Plant tiny, American flags in no wind, in his
Coma, his Asia.   But no.   At the end his face

In the newspapers smeared with rain still
Looked delicately cross with something, almost
Childish, tired.   The waitress in this truck stop
Believes, with Da Vinci, that the world will end

In fires, storms, and silence.   This is Nebraska,
Where the cattle across from us look up quietly,
Chewing sideways with abrupt motions.   I watch
A whole weed, roots and all, disappear.   It was

Da Vinci who knew all the muscles in the human face.

Story

I know the white wedding dress is suicidal.
I know how the bride trembles, putting it on.

And tonight the groom is pissing into some shrubs
behind a tavern.   It is late, and he thinks

Of twin sores riding the rump of a horse
As it is being whipped into a slow trot,

And of how the driver nods to the butcher, who waves
Back after smearing his apron with the blood

Of hogs.   And now the butcher takes one long drink
Of black wine, and calculates how many new flies

Will hatch in the park, if there are three thousand
Flies in each pond, if there are thirty ponds.

Then he calculates how many each carp will eat,
If there are fifty carp in each pond.   It passes

The day, he thinks, this calculating the flies.
Still, it is the butcher, slicing off his index finger

At the knuckle, who keeps death away from this poem
Long enough for the bride to marry.   Long enough

For the horse to die, two months later, standing still
In a slaughterhouse.   And long enough for the flies

To swarm over the meat in their loud, black weddings.

Ice

Walking home, I see the last ice
Of winter crusting the yards, and here
The pale, twisted limbs of a doll left out
When the children stopped playing, and
Went indoors, and the first, soft snows
Came down in the air like stilled speech.
The houses pass on both sides of me. Each
With an aunt who is ill, or with a father
Who has become, at this age, a secret
Even he cannot know, and who waits to be
Told what it is, or how its story,
Without him, can go on. At home,
I drop a cube of ice into a glass
Of clear ouzo, and swallow, and see
Nothing amusing in the way the leaves
Have held on to their branches all winter,
Or in the way these trees keep standing
For death, in the book about death.
The boy I shot eight ball with last night
In the pool hall told me he'd got syphilis
Again, and from the same woman. When she
Came, sitting on his lap and still dressed
In his car, he said her eyes were almost
Closed, like a hen's at nightfall—the skin
Over them pale and so thin he remembered
Tracing things on paper, as a child.
He laughed, and shrugged it off . . .
I could have told him that the skin
Around the body is fragrant, thin as paper,
And fatal. Instead, I listened only to
The soft click of billiards, and soft curses . . .
He asked me what I did, and when I told him
He frowned, and said at home his father
Thought most books were bad, and burned
The ones he disagreed with, on the lawn.

We both laughed, though it was colder,
And along the bar now most of the men
Had paid up and gone out with no music
On their lips. Each face, tense with its
Secret, was outliving music, and I knew how
The lights in the farmhouses along the river
Would go out quietly and suddenly as they
Arrived. I knew how their door sills
Would scrape at a last step—how each of us
Would come alone to the end of a different
Story, and how we would not come back,
Not even in the frosted breath of children
Picking their way home from school, in winter—
And how they would yell to one another, even then,
Never dreaming we could hear their cries.

Adah

I can remember the almost private outburst
Of rain on the tin sheds:
A sound as precise as a small fire taking hold
Of its kindling;
Or, when the rain stopped, the drone of flies
And their shining—
And how the horses outside
Would lift and drop a hoof in the pasture
As they grazed, heads down,
Or flicked their ears back . . .
And the skin inside their ears resembling a human's,
But softer, really, than anyone's
I have ever met, or will meet now.
Not even
The balding widow mesmerized by fans
And by Sundays,
Who waits all night now for sleep
Can do without counting horses and flies
Until she is alone,
Before sleep, and lying in the stiffened,
Almost righteous position that pain allows her.
And as if prayer could collapse
The tool shed and split the shining anvil
Inside it,
She will not do anything as precise and blasphemous
As pray anymore.
She will only listen, and think,
Maybe, of horses,
And do as little as horses do,
Which is her privilege, as it is the river's,
Or the heavy woods, which do nothing.
As even the mottled grass
In which the kidnappers smothered the child
Does nothing, does not even conceal the place
Now that they have

Gone on, without speaking, into a stand of elms
And into history.
Though not before they threatened a farm wife
Who was able to sift strychnine into their lunch
And serve it to them
With a tight smile and a forehead as cool
To the touch as it is now,
When she remembers it all before sleep,
And remembers
Trailing them at a distance until they
Both fell.
And beside a field of white stubble
And a road she had always lived near,
And always would live near,
She watched them without any curiosity.
She thought they sounded
Like two syllables that could not find their
Proper places
When someone is trying to say a word.
It was hot,
They were human.
She felt her thin dress aging in the sun.

Edward Hopper, *Hotel Room*, 1931

The young woman is just sitting on the bed,
Looking down.   The room is so narrow she keeps
Her elbows tucked in, resting, on her bare thighs,
As if that could help.

She is wearing, now, only an orange half-slip
That comes down as far as her waist, but does not
Console her body, which fails.
Which must sleep, by now, apart from everyone.
And her face, in shadow,
Is more silent than this painting, or any
Painting: it feels like the sad, blank hull
Of a ship is passing, slowly, the stones of a wharf,
Though there is no ocean for a thousand miles,
And outside this room I can imagine only Kansas:
Its wheat, and blackening silos, and, beyond that,
The plains that will stare back at you until
The day your mother, kneeling in fumes
On a hardwood floor, begins to laugh out loud.
When you visit her, you see the same, faint grass
Around the edge of the asylum, and a few moths,
White and flagrant, against the wet brick there,
Where she has gone to live.   She never
Recognizes you again.

You sell the house, and auction off each thing
Inside the house, until
You have a satchel, a pair of black, acceptable
Shoes, and one good flowered dress.   There is a check
Between your hands and your bare knees for all of it—
The land and the wheat that never cared who
Touched it, or why.

*

You think of curves, of the slow, mild arcs
Of harbors in California: Half Moon Bay,

Malibu, names that seen to undress
When you say them, beaches that stay white
Until you get there. Still, you're only thirty-five,
And that is not too old to be a single woman,
Traveling west with a purse in her gray lap
Until all of Kansas dies inside her stare . . .

*

But you never moved, never roused yourself
To go down Grain Street to the sobering station,
Never gazed out at the raw tracks, and waited
For the train that pushed its black smoke up
Into the sky like something important . . .

And now it is too late for you. Now no one,
Turning his collar up against the cold
To walk past the first, full sunlight flooding
The white sides of houses, knows why
You've kept on sitting here for forty years—alone,
Almost left out of the picture, half undressed.

To a Woman Glancing Up
from the River

On either bank,
There is a brief silence just before dawn,
And a light turned to the color of iron.
The night, rising,
Is a man stepping back from a campfire and into
The woods—
Though by the time you can see those trees,
Oaks and elms, he is entirely gone,
And gone in exactly the way he desires, without
Tracks, or singing.
Years later,
You will believe that every
Disappearance must have this secrecy
Inside it,
As if a breath were held behind a doll's bitter face,
Bloating its skin.
Now, you watch bark drift past you to join
The smells rising off the river all summer:
Steel, and hogs,
The small fires giving out into smoke
And blue coals.
When your husband disappeared, it looked
As if he'd died; his shirts
Still on hangers,
And his boots still holding the delicate shapes
Of his ankles.
He simply strolled out to talk to someone
In the dusk,
And became the dusk.
It took him five minutes.
Afternoons, you drank in each bar,
And cursed even the white moths under the bridges.
You met other men.
You slept alone, or not alone, or you

Did not sleep.
You moved to the edge of the town
And let your hair grow out.
At night, you listened to the wind drying the weeds.
You spoke, finally, only to clouds and trees
Along the road.
You stopped believing in sorrow.
There is a short silence just before dawn
While a flat sun comes
Over the river,
Until it fires, as if from underneath, the face
Of that water—
Which will not be troubled by your own—
And though you stare into it for a long time,
It slips past you;
The sun rises,
The water ripples and its wide back fills with light.

A Pool of Light

—for my grandparents

1. *Silk*

The body sprawls over the couch—
His bruised face looking
As if it listens to all voices at once, now,
Though in the end he died hearing cars sweep past him
On the street,
And did not think they sounded
Like rain, or like anyone's breath.
What is left here
Is only the solitude in the scent of a woman.
She is alone,
She is sitting on the edge of the bed, dazed.
Earlier, she told them all to get out,
She told them she would undress him
By herself,
And then she sat with him for hours,
Bathing his body in warm water,
And waiting for it to come back to her.
Nothing happened: the night
Was like the nights in small towns she had lived in,
Where she knew it would go on raining,
And something inside her, a stillness in the spine,
A cough, would not change.
And later, when the stars appeared one by one
In the black sky,
She was ashamed,
And she did not want to touch him anymore.
She remembered lying back once
On the cool floor of a dance hall—
It was summer,
It was Sunday afternoon, and no one was there.
Beside them, a shaft of light held up the dust
For their inspection,

But they did not see it, then.
And when she cried out?
A sound inside her throat like cranes in a wet,
Black field!

Outside the house,
A thin moon.

*

When I come back in a year,
There are rags stuffed in the windows.
I clear my throat in the cold
And keep watching: soon,
She is pulling on her boots and getting ready
To go out.
She has been drinking gin,
And she can almost feel something come near,
Something she has been listening for.
But that will not happen today.
Today, she is singular.
Today she is rare silk.
She takes the thin, gray arm of the wind
In her arm,
And steadies it.

2.

Skinny ghost, this is the laughter
You threw under the bridge
To no one
When the water swirled, and you felt cold.
This is old news
They use to wrap fish, and flowers,
And shattered dishes in.
Or, this is simply what happens when you
Outlive yourself,
And what matters, finally, on long walks
In winter, is a good coat.
And while the same white clouds kept massing

In the painting above your bed,
And your hair was wet,
I tried to imagine those last days
That paralyzed the left side of your body.
All I could think of was an oak struck once
By lightning in our yard;
How each year it kept sending out
Frail, white shoots.
In the end, you died in a coma,
While outside the hospital, sunset
Was a pool of light that rotted away
Streets, and houses.
In the end,
It didn't matter what I thought of.

The Grass

I dreamed our two skulls were filling with bees.
Waking, it is not true.

But if I have to witness anything today,
I think it will be only this tough grass
Beside the pond, this womanly hair

That won't die.

I can still hear the thin music of flies
Above the water,
And today we came up from the long fields
And ate, and lay down
In the shadows of oaks . . .Asleep, her strong body
Is a temple that casts out the unbeliever,
The leper, the heretic.
Such trust in the sun . . .
She dreams easily . . .

But I think of each muscle it must have taken
For her body to walk through cold sunlight once,
To find a service station, a bathroom mirror,
To comb her hair and feel it bleed,
And say nothing.
Now I am hearing the wind in that bare place,

And though I am ashamed to be here,
I must watch her ankles
Crossing the hard mud and ice of a farm yard
In winter, ten years ago.
She is nineteen.
And last night a drunk soldier beat her up.
Does anyone else need to see these bruises?
They are only the hush of blood over a body
That wanted to be music,
A spine's singing.

I turn to the witnesses here:
This matted grass in which she must have sat down
To rest,
The warm snow in patches,
And one wren that goes on cleaning
Its breast feathers with its beak.

Ten years. I close my eyes.
I vanish into the broken glass on the roadside
Where you walked.

I sit down in our quiet house, and wait.

PART THREE

Words for the Axe

Each day I go further into the woods.
They fall before me like a road
Without stars, and without a curve.
It goes on the ocean, now.

And at night I fly so deeply into myself
I become still. I shine under the moon
Like the lost child you glimpse
Beneath the ice on the one day of the year
You decide to go skating.

Whoever it is that holds me, my one friend,
Is only a flowing of blood:
And blood spreads like branches in summer,
The leaves shading a house where the people
Sleep, and the birds keep their distance
From other birds, and it is the world.

It *is* the world—   and where the ground was hard,
I helped bury its dead,
Hacking past rocks and roots until
I found a place, even for them.
There is no moral to my story.
From the outset, I gleamed, like a sea.

My Only Photograph of Weldon Kees

—for D.J.

10 p.m., the river thinking
Of its last effects,
The bridges empty.   I think
You would have left the party late,

Declining a ride home.
And no one notices, now,
The moist hat brims
Between the thumbs of farmers

In Beatrice, Nebraska.
The men in their suits,
Ill fitting, bought on sale . . .
The orange moon of foreclosures.

And abandoning the car!
How you soloed, finally,
Lending it the fabulous touch
Of your absence.

You'd call that style—
To stand with an unlit cigarette
In one corner of your mouth,
Admiring the sun on Alcatraz.

The Blue Hatband

Sometimes, even in the middle of a conversation
In a bar, even at noon, I turn away.
I stare out at a single brick in a wall,
And a woman without a mouth begins to speak.

I listen, but it is like listening to paper
When a bird walks over it: someone scrapes
Against that brick in a speech that is not human—
And, hearing it, I forget which names I love.

My friends and what I said today mean less
Than a pale blue hatband on a man climbing,
Slowly, the stairs of a building in 1930 . . .
That man arrested Anna Akhmatova's only son.

If she was silenced later, and if she stood
In lines with packages outside each prison,
I hope her anger will become a hollow place
In an elm where lovers hide notes, the snows come,

And the parks are full of skaters.   But I think
That Anna Akhmatova has not slept for years,
And now she is awake beyond music, beyond shoes
That button up the sides of each thin ankle,

Beyond her face that lacks teeth, eyes, a mouth—
A face that can stare back, even now, in Ohio,
Until I doze on this train, and let the fields pass,
Their weeds the vague, gray flags of childhood.

*

But while I sleep, I dream St. Petersburg
Out of each book, and they start shooting students
In Ohio, again.   Her hair, in each jail, grows whiter . . .
And when I wake, I have no right to speak.

43

*

Anna Akhmatova, watching blood cover the lips
Of horses, remembered her son's skin as snow,
Sky, the shattered porcelain on a roadside—
As the white skins of swans drying over her head,

Once, in a market. Even now, when the dead wake
Inside her blood, she approaches that butcher,
She raises a finger to haggle over such meat,
She stares straight at him, and turns to air.

But the butcher looks up, into his unlit, empty shop.

For Miguel Hernández in His Sleep
and in His Sickness: Spring, 1942, Madrid

You have slept for two days now,
And still you do not want
To die in here.
If you had a choice,
You would lie without thoughts in the long grass,
Where the grass is whitest—
Each blade of it a flame that says nothing,
That loves nothing . . .
If you had a choice,
You would be done with loving forever.
You would walk toward a loud square in Madrid,
And lie down, unnoticed, in the twisting shade
Of a black tree, and sleep.
Or maybe you would only pretend to sleep—
Maybe you would close your eyes in the sun,
And let the flies settle on your lips,
And listen to the threadbare blood rushing
Inside your veins;
Maybe you would let the stray goats nuzzle your hands,
Since there is nothing shameful
Under the sky.
But on the third day
Without food, or prayers, or water,
You would see your first and last words grow still
As a glass of wine in a woman's hand:
She would be sitting in a café, alone,
Not noticing you, not
Hearing your breath become quick and shallow—
Until finally you would let it all out in one hard laugh
That withers quickly
Into the noise of the street.
And without breath,
You would become the street:
You would become these goats braying,

The scrape of soldiers,
A girl's laugh inside a bar . . .
I could visit you years from now
In these bricks and these black shops and even
In this shattered glass that no one cleans up,
That shines in the sun—
That remains
When everyone goes home to curse, or sleep,
Or lie awake between his own two hands.
And who knows how this night will end?
The grass stirs once and stills
Outside the prison.
You think no one is worth his life, and the stars,
Even the rare, white ones that are so useless
To men and women,
Show up again above you.

For Zbigniew Herbert, Summer, 1971, Los Angeles

No matter how hard I listen, the wind speaks
One syllable, which has no comfort in it—
Only a rasping of air through the dead elm.
*

Once a poet told me of his friend who was torn apart
By two pigs in a field in Poland. The man
Was a prisoner of the Nazis, and they watched,
He said, with interest and a drunken approval . . .
If terror is a state of complete understanding,

Then there was probably a point at which the man
Went mad, and felt nothing, though certainly
He understood everything that was there: after all,
He could see blood splash beneath him on the stubble,
He could hear singing float toward him from the barracks.
*

And though I don't know much about madness,
I know it lives in the thin body like a harp
Behind the rib cage.   It makes it painful to move.
And when you kneel in madness your knees are glass,
And so you must stand up again with great care.
*

Maybe this wind was what he heard in 1941.
Maybe I have raised a dead man into this air,
And now I will have to bury him inside my body,
And breathe him in, and do nothing but listen—
Until I hear the black blood rushing over
The stone of my skull, and believe it is music.

But some things are not possible on the earth.
And that is why people make poems about the dead.
And the dead watch over them, until they are finished:
Until their hands feel like glass on the page,
And snow collects in the blind eyes of statues.

García Lorca: A Photograph of the Granada Cemetery, 1966

The men who killed poetry
Hated silence . . .Now they have plenty.
In the ossuary at Granada
There are over four thousand calm skulls
Whitening; the shrubs are in leaf
Behind the bones.
And if anyone tries to count spines
He can feel his own scalp start to crawl
Back to its birthplace.

Once, I gave you a small stone I respected.
When I turned it over in the dawn,
After staying up all night,
Its pale depths
Resembled the tense face of Lorca
Spitting into an empty skull.
Why did he do that?
Someone should know.
Someone should know by now that the stone
Was only an amulet to keep the dead away.

And though your long bones
Have nothing to do with Lorca, or those deaths
Forty years ago, in Spain,
The trees fill with questions, and summer.
He would not want, tonight, another elegy.
He would want me to examine the marriage of wings
Beneath your delicate collar bones:
They breathe,
The ribs of your own poems breathe.

And here is our dark house at the end of the lane.
And here is the one light we have kept on all year
For no one, or Lorca,

And now he comes toward it—
With the six bulletholes in his chest,
Walking lightly
So he will not disturb the sleeping neighbors,
Or the almonds withering in their frail arks
Above us.
He does not want to come in.
He stands embarrassed under the street lamp
In his rumpled suit . . .

Snow, lullabye, anvil of bone
That terrifies the blacksmith in his sleep,

Your house is breath.

The Wish to Be Picked Clean

I still oversleep these winter mornings;
I still can't decide.
Last night,
I desired only
A stillness in the wake of each thing:
The air held inside a dead spider on the sill,
Or inside a shell washed up this morning;
Or even the air of a struck chord
When the pianist seems to lean over, slightly,
As if he strains to hear a note just under
His own held breath.
I wanted, once, to be picked clean by music,
By wind, by sunlight.
I would stand outside in the winter dusk,
I would think
Of those extinct Scottish poets
Who placed stones on their bare chests
And then laid down in snow each night until
The right poem came.
They praised, always, the hard ways of their Lord;
Their grins frightened even
Their wives . . .
It took me fifteen years to learn
How not to pray,
And tonight I toast a blind, black man
With a cane,
Who I met, once, in Louisville.
Whose socks were unmatching: one a fading gold,
One white.
It was humid in the park,
And he sat there,
Smiling at each thing I said.
I thought he liked the feeling of the sun
On his face, or on his hands,
Or that he liked my company.

I learned, later, that he was simply terrified,
And that a gang of boys had crept up, earlier,
With sticks—
I was too young, then;
I was nothing, then,
And in the morning he was not there.
I still wake up with no beliefs,
But looking out this year at the brown grass,
I think that frail man is dead by now,
And though I do not know
If the veins on the backs of his hands
Were sacred, they stood out
While he listened,
As if his blood was thinking.
If I could imagine him now, picked clean
And without pain
By the salts of his own body—
As the top of his cane must have been polished
For years by the sweat
From both his thumbs,
It would be easy,
It would be a wind no thicker than your wrist
Over this page, or the music of wind
When you hear it, suddenly,
Sitting alone in a cafeteria in Louisville—
While the river there, the glittering Ohio,
Goes on with what it does,
And each night, over it, the stars
Are bright and deep, and no one speaks to you.

PART FOUR

Lost Fan, Hotel Californian,
Fresno, 1923

In Fresno it is 1923, and your shy father
Has picked up a Chinese fan abandoned
Among the corsages crushed into the dance floor.
On it, a man with scrolls is crossing a rope bridge
Over gradually whitening water.
If you look closely you can see brush strokes intended
To be trout.
You can see that the whole scene
Is centuries older
Than the hotel, or Fresno in the hard glare of morning.
And the girl
Who used this fan to cover her mouth
Or breasts under the cool brilliance
Of chandeliers
Is gone on a train sliding along tracks that are
Pitted with rust.
All this is taking her south,
And as your father opens the fan now you can see
The rope bridge tremble and the lines of concentration
Come over the face of this thin scholar
Who makes the same journey alone each year
Into the high passes,
Who sleeps on the frozen ground, hearing the snow
Melt around him as he tries hard
Not to be involved with it, not to be
Awakened by a spring that was never meant
To include him—
And though he hears the geese racket above him
As if a stick were held flat against

A slat fence by a child running past a house for sale;
And though he has seen his sons' kites climb the air
With clumsy animals, dragons and oxen,
Painted over them in great detail,
He does not care if kites continue to stiffen
Each year against the sky, the sun.
When he lays
His one good ear to the ground he thinks
He is the conclusion of something argued over all night,
He thinks of his skull as a drum with a split skin
Left out in the rain,
Washed continually but not about to be picked up
As someone picks up a fan even, out of curiosity,
Revolves it slowly,
And now, gently closes it.
And though flies cover the chandeliers this morning,
The new seeds steam underground,
The snow melts,
The mist rises off the thawing river,
And the girl wakens in her berth—
Her face cradling a slight frown,
As if she had just outgrown all dancing,
And turned serious, like the sky.

Some Ashes Drifting Above
Piedra, California

There is still one field I can love;
There is still a little darkness in each furrow
And each stump.
Behind it
You can sit down and begin to doubt
Even the hair on the backs of your hands—
And what you see now is nothing:
It is only
The scrubbed, wooden sink inside this shack
Abandoned by farm workers,
Or, above a kitchen window, only a strip of curtain
Which is the color of no flag
And no country, though once it meant *night*—
And so the occupant stared out at the sky whitening
Into each dawn—
At all the withheld information
Which is sky,
And thought if he worked all day to shovel
Thirty acres of vines
Without once looking up into those torn clouds,
If he could sweat past such insolence into nightfall,
And ignore that, too, until he saw her
Turning from a bath,
Her skin suddenly
There, and darker than he could have believed—
As if night had entered the dusk
Of her body . . .
So their eyes and mouths opened, then.

And now,
If we listen for their laughter,
Which vanished fifteen years ago
Into the cleft wood of these boards,
Into the night and the rain,

It will sound like cold jewels spilling together,
It will sound like snow . . .
We will never have any money, either,
And we will go on staring past the sink,
Past the curtain,
And into a field which is not even white anymore,
Not even an orchard,
But simply this mud,
And always,
Over that, a hard sky.
And what I have to tell you now is only
The salt that ripens in our passing, and
Overwhelms us:
How I heard, once,
Of two lovers, who
Naked, and for a joke,
Tied themselves together with cast off clothes
And leaped into a canal—
Where the current held them under a whole hour.
I thought, then,
How each of them must have said all that can
Be said
Between a man and a woman—
As they fought each other to breathe,
Or, which is the same thing,
To be whole, and lonely again.
But I was wrong:
They only stiffened, and there were no words left
Inside them—
The man lay face down in the stillness;
The woman faced the sky.
Bobbing in the thick grass beside the banks,
Their arms whitened around each other for three days
In the stale water . . .
Now they are these words.
And now, if I strike a match
To offer you
This page burned all the way

Into their silences,
Take it—
While your hair dies a little more
Into the day,
While the sun rises,
These two will be ashes in the palm of my hand,
Stirring a little and about to drift
Easily away, without comment,
On the wind.

Magnolia

If I knew a way, I would tell you.
The man who threw a bottle from a passing car
At a young couple on a porch simply
Disappears into the night.

Still, I have my reasons for coming back
To this town, to these
Bright initials carved into an oak tree.
It is in leaf, and just now
It is shading a bare place in the park where
Two lovers are lying. Sunlight
And shadow dapple the woman's skirt
While she tries to figure out something with a stick—
Tracing the problem on the gray earth until
All of the lines intersect like a web, or a nest.
The man beside her is pretending to be asleep.
He looks pale and naïve with his eyes closed.
He looks as if he is remembering being young,
And an addict, because he is.
At 19, how it made the sun of damp places
Darken a little.
But not enough.
It was never enough,
And there was always this waiting for someone
To show up.
But before the singing began in his veins,
And engraved them again,
There were even a few pure moments,
More honest than clouds, or sunlight, or any
Blossoming thing beside him,
While he waited, and while he remembered
The hand of a friend growing cold in his hand—
How they were just watching
A concert together, and how
His friend died like that, casually,

As if he had decided not to listen anymore.
He left him lying there on the grass in Golden Gate Park,
And walked for an hour through Flieschacker Zoo.

I suppose he likes this oak tree, now, because
It doesn't judge him, and because it seems only
Amazed to be here, in leaf, and still standing.
I won't judge him, either.
Caught always in the spring of my 33rd year,
I hope I will not have to judge anyone
Singular and hopeless in the salt of his dying.
If I knew a way, I would tell him.
Though I would not tell him
That I died listening
To my own blood sing in the unheard registers
Of ice, and flowers—   and lost it, finally,
In the most difficult passage.
If I knew a way, I would come up
The long, graying grass of this hill, and tell him,
And hold the thin shoulders of this man and this
Woman, who are ashamed, by now,
To *have* shoulders,
And tell them that it doesn't matter, that feeling
Your skin grow cold, and sudden,
Doesn't matter.

I would lie to them both, even now.
Because in the end, it was humiliating.
In the end, I was simplified, like a wild,
White Magnolia blossom I once saw. It was turning
Slowly brown in the hand of a schoolboy
While he kept staring patiently out
The rain streaked windows of a bus.

For a Ghost Who Once Placed
Bets in the Park

To become as pure as I am,
You will have to sit all day in a small park
Blackening one end of Fowler, California.
You will have to stare steadily past the still swings
Ignored by children,
And listen to the perfect Spanish of a car thief
Who knows he will never be caught,
Who drinks wine alone as he mumbles his innocence
To a dead sister.
You will have to study the muscles in the face of a woman
Sickened by no one, or summer, who pulls a shopping cart
Behind her with a black, gloved hand.
Each day she pauses before going up
The slope of the hill.
She complains to her three distinct, personal gods,
She wets her lips,
She almost dozes on her feet.
The car thief takes a long sip of wine and watches her,
And watches the shadows falling over the swings,
And the shrubs, and the sparrows.
Again today I bet against the shadows and lost:
They lengthened
For hours until their immaculate shade
Contradicted the sky.
And though it is the same sky the two lovers sat under,
They were so undone by their own glances,
By the white silks of their flesh,
I almost believed I was wrong about this place.
In my silence, of course, I bet against them,
And bet too hard.
As summer worried the lace from ferns,
And as summer nights rotted the eyes out of moths,
In August,
I watched the boy stifle a yawn,

I watched them quarrel.
Soon the girl was just something thin in a blue dress,
Sitting alone in shade.
The woman in black gloves is too old to care
About shade now.
She stands out on the sidewalk and lets the heat
Pour through her, and lets the muscles of her heart
Learn what the sun can do.
And if she laughs,
It is because the humiliation of sunlight
Has cured her body of every dignity,
And made it useless again.
To become this pure, this empty,
You will have to sit beside me for hours,
And hear the car thief explain his crime over and over,
Or watch this woman pray against the muscles
Inside her own mind,
And then follow her up the hill
Until she disappears,
And you find only yourself staring back
At the green shadows spreading through the park, and the
   shrubs
Refusing to die, and the three motionless swings.

Overhearing the Dollmaker's Ghost
on the Riverbank

The Missouri is only a mile from this place,
But I haven't seen it glint through the bridge railings
For two months, its back careless, flat,
And unaging.
Seen for the first time it moves faster
Than you expected, like the back
Of an animal you glimpse from the highway
But can't identify.
And once, on its banks near Canada,
I saw a bear
Moving quickly through goldenrod glance up once
And judge me.   Then it
Walked off with a sort of arrogant peacefulness
In each stride.
And held for a moment in the contempt
Of its stare, hearing
The wind over the blind stones,
I learned only what I knew:
That the sun would go down,
The bread I was eating would be water,
And the river would flow under the creaking pilings
Until another shack came riding high
In the spring floods.
And trapped twice by rising water,
I was lucky enough to crawl into a cave an share it
With scorpions, and admire their selfishness,
And bless power.

*

But nothing could laugh fear out of my house—
It lived in the brown shoes I had to put on
Each morning, and in the cancer blooming under
My father's lapel, and in my mother taking in laundry
All through World War I.

Fear was curious: it asked me
My name, asked me to sit down and showed me all the tools
In the shed, and asked if I knew their uses.
And I lied because I needed the money;
And because they said someone had to place buttons
Carefully in the skulls of dolls,
And do this over and over,
I was a dollmaker.
Until each doll grew luminous, and each inhaled
My gaze. And then I gave those eyes
Everything they asked,
Which was nothing.
Which was thirty years.

*

And once, driving home, I saw a torn mattress
High on a riverbank, and wondered
Who had slept there, what love stains
Might be drying on it in the late afternoon sun,
And what lice might be sleeping inside it,
Unaware that their hosts had moved elsewhere.
And so strapped it over the roof of my car,
And got it home,
And sat there on it, drinking wine and grinning.
And it was my wide grin and all 29 teeth
That remembered who I had slept with
In 1947, and who was
Blinded at random on the street by acid thrown
Into her eyes,
And why the sky is for sale.
Because in the end it wasn't a bear
Or a mattress on a raft that saved me.
It wasn't my body
Like a graveyard glimpsed inside a sunset
While someone is writing a letter;
It wasn't even my disappearance,
Or my cousins dredging the water.
It was the river moving all night under me,

It was the fast, black river
That didn't care what I did,
That slowed when I looked at it closely
And carried twigs and shoes
And a rank stench like unwashed human hair and flesh
Past the abandoned freight yards of the Missouri,
And past the white hair of women who go mad on its banks,
Watching for my body to surface in the warming water.

And now I will sit here all night carving
At a dry stick of wood,
Ignoring whoever it is
That gets up slowly and walks back
To his car, and rolls up the windows—
So he won't hear the grass dying around me
In late August—
And drives away.

To My Ghost Reflected in the Auxvasse River

I'm tired of praising the dead
Tired of ghosts.
I am just sitting in my yard, watching
Thin clouds move above me,
And the grasses all bending in one direction.
This wind has no friend but me;
It is Spring,
And I am addressing you, Spirit,
Because the wheat ripens for no one,
Not for the sky,
Not even for you,
And you, who do not believe in words,
Care less for my life than for a broken comb you've left
In a movie theater, or in a bar.
Each day at noon
I used to close my eyes,
And lie alone in the dark, listening.
And you never spoke,
Never uttered the thin prayer that was me.
Or on the long bridges when I drove to work,
You would stare into the river
Until you made yourself think of nothing.
And when you found you could do it,
You were thrilled,
You were like a spider
Moving laboriously, and without thoughts, over a bead
Of water shining in its web.
You stayed out later, and later.
You loved knives, bars, drugs, music.
When you would turn on the radio
And dance alone, in the kitchen
Of the diner,
I kept sweeping.
You have become pure, finally.

You have become that silence just under the water
Where the river turns brown, and slows,
And a stillness rides alone
Over that place—
And I just drive past it, now.
If only I could reach in and pull you out,
Or if only you were a fish,
And then, if you did not speak to me,
As a fish did once, in a dream,
I would slice you up to the stomach and slap
Your head against stone,
And make you flesh,
Even while these flies dance on the rocks.
But I am a stranger, I will pass,
And always, when I bend to drink
From this place, I come up with nothing, with
Broken water, a fine
Trembling in my hands,
Which must be you.

Blue Stones

—for my son, Nicholas

I suspect
They will slide me onto a cold bed,
A bed that has been brought in,
Out of the night
And past the fraying brick of the warehouse,
Where maybe a workman took an afternoon nap,
And woke staring up
At what sky he could see through one window.
But if he kept staring,
And thought that the bed took its gray color
From the sky, and kept watching that sky
Even after he had finished his cigarette,
He might learn
How things outlive us.
And maybe he would be reminded that the body, too
Is only a thing, a joke it kept trying to tell us,
And now the moment for hearing it
Is past.
All I will have to decide, then,
Is how to behave during
Those last weeks, when the drawers
Of the dresser remain closed,
And the mirror is calm, and reflects nothing,
And outside, tangled
In the hard branches,
The moon appears.
I see how poor it is,
How it owns nothing.
I look at it a long time, until
I feel empty, as if I had travelled on foot
For three days, and become simple,
The way light was simple on the backs

Of horses as my father approached them,
Quietly, with a bridle.
My father thought dying
Was like standing trial for crimes
You could not remember.
Then someone really does throw
The first stone.
It is blue,
And seems to be made of the sky itself.
The breath goes out of you.
Tonight, the smoke holds still
Against the hills and trees outside this town,
And there is no hope
Of acquittal.

*

But *you*? Little believer, little
Straight, unbroken, and tireless thing,
Someday, when you are twenty-four and walking through
The streets of a foreign city, Stockholm,
Or Trieste,
Let me go with you a little way,
Let me be that stranger you won't notice,
And when you turn and enter a bar full of young men
And women, and your laughter rises,
Like the stones of a path up a mountain,
To say that no one has died,
I promise I will not follow.
I will cross at the corner in my gray sweater.
I will not have touched you,
As I did, for so many years,
On the hair and the left shoulder.
I will silence my hand that wanted to.
I will put it in my pocket, and let it clutch
The cold, blue stones they give you,
As a punishment,
After you have lived.

The Spirit Says,
You are Nothing:

Because you haven't praised anything in months,
You walk down to the river and study one ripple
Above a dead tree
Until it is almost dark enough
For the moon to whiten it,
But it does not,
And so you put your hand out,
Palm open,
And then you feel, or you begin to feel,
A thin line of ants hesitate
Before running over it,
And you think how
The thread of worry running through a human voice
Halts when a syllable freezes, then goes on,
Alone.   You remember
Overhearing two voices speak softly
In a motel room.
Outside, it was 1975,
And cars sighed past weeds, and fields.
You think now they were only
A man and a woman consoling each other
Because they had both
Lived out their lives, and there was no point
Anymore, worth arguing, even if once
There was something, no money, or a daughter
Staying out all night even on the blackest night
Of summer, and coming home
Whitened and final as snow in the back seat
Of a convertible—
The car abandoned, by now, to the sky and the sun—
But no, they
Were just consoling each other
For being who they were,

And because they could not change,
Not now, into
Anything else.
And because one day one of them will simply look over
To see if the water on the stove
Is boiling, and if it is clear, finally,
Of the gray, shifting sky it had reflected
A moment ago,
And then he, or she, will be alone—
Though the sun might move to illuminate
A spiked clematis on the windowsill,
Which will be too revealing.
And whoever is left
Will begin to know what it is like
To take one step slowly backward;
To be without a voice to sort the mind
As it begins, now, to flare like the horns
Of a marching band coming up the street under
The elms;

To feel a slight wind stirring the hair at the back
Of the neck . . .

To stand there.

*

By now you are lying so still
You think you can rise up, as I can,
Without a body,
And go unseen over the still heads of grasses,
And enter the house
Where your wife will not look up from the letter
She is writing,
And your son goes on sleeping—
A thimble of light spilling into the darkness.
But you do not move.   And this
Is about stillness, now:
How you remember strolling alone, at seventeen,

Through the dusk of each street,
How you liked the wind reddening the face
Of a drunk, who,
In the last days of his alcohol, reeled
And stared back at you,
And held your gaze.
How all you remember of New York is
That man,
Who would not have read this poem,
Or any poem,
And who once dreamed
That a speck of white paint on a subway platform
Would outlast
Everyone he knew.

*

But you were young, and you had
Plenty of time:
Going west,

You slept on the train and did not smile.
Under you the plains widened, and turned silver.

You slept with your mouth open.

You were nothing,
You were snow falling through the ribs
Of the dead.

You were all I had.